Effective Time
Management Strategies
Copyright 2013

Wayne Sutton

www.CoachingWithWayne.com

Table of Contents

Introduction

There are so many distractions in today's world of business technology that few people manage their time effectively. Cell phones, FaceBook, Twitter, email, online meetings, software updates, the telephone, conference calling, and online bill pay, all created to make our work more productive, can make time much less manageable if not used wisely .

As people try to get more activities crammed into their lives and more business accomplished, scheduling, managing, and prioritizing tasks has become even more critical.

There is a broad difference between quantity and quality when it comes to managing the use of our time. Few business owners spend a fraction of time managing their own time compared to watching the activity of employee's time.

Imagine the feeling at the end of the day, knowing you accomplished everything you set out to do and made the best use of your time.

Imagine having a plan for each day that actually worked!

This book will give you the strategies and tools you need to get the fulfillment you should be receiving from each day.

Chapter 1. The Secret of Getting More Time

Everyday people are heard saying I wish I had more time. They run through from task to task and event to event at light speed, trying to find ways to do and accomplish more.

Some people seem to accomplish far more than others in their day, week, and lifetime. Benjamin Franklin was a successful author, politician, scientist, philosopher, printer, inventor, activist, and diplomat. His accomplishments are astounding. He was a scientist known for his theories and discoveries and gained the recognition of fellow scientists and intellectuals. He was a political writer and activist, and served as a diplomat during the American Revolution. He was a newspaper editor, self published author. PostMaster General, and started the first American library. His credits go on and on.

Benjamin Franklin is even credited for the statement; 'Time is money.' How did he find the time?

The good news is there is no more time! How can that be good news?

In this respect, the playing field is level.
- Everyone gets the same twenty-four hours in a day.
- Your competition has no more hours in a day than you.
- The richest man cannot buy even one more minute of time in a day!
- You can only manage yourself and activities more effectively.

In a typical forty-hour workweek, it's estimated that the average person spends:

> 1.7 hours looking for things
> 1.0 hour rescheduling appointments and tasks
> 1.4 hours wasted because of rescheduled appointments and tasks
> 2.2 hours wasted because of disorganization and lack of priority

This is a total of more than 6 hours wasted due to poor planning and a lack of organization.
When people are asked why they are not organized, the number one reason given is:

'I don't have the time.'

The fact is, people choose to be disorganized. Most people could save this wasted time by spending just two hours a week organizing and planning. In just two hours of planning, you could free an additional three to four hours every week of prime time.

Effective Time Management is about behavioral change. Learning how to spend more time acting instead of reacting. The skills described herein will help you become better organized and manage time more effectively, which will increase productivity, but only if you adapt the behavioral changes as outlined throughout this book.

The fact that most organizations do not have a time management program in place suggests that they do not feel that this is an issue that needs to be addressed. However, nothing affects the ability of a company to function and be productive more than the ability of its employees to use organizational skills in order to save time during the business day. Companies must take action in order to encourage their employees to become more skilled in organization and time management. Even if you are an extremely organized person, all of your efforts will be wasted if your employees are not picking up where you leave off. There are several things you can do as an owner or manager to encourage your employees to become more efficient managers of time.

First, think of your employees' time as an asset. It is a tangible asset that is worth a great deal of money and must be dealt with accordingly. Your job is to mange this incredibly valuable asset. You cannot assume that your employees know how to regulate their use of time on their own. As a business owner or manager, it is your job to use the 40 hours per week an employee gives you in the most efficient manner possible.

Next, when you are hiring new employees, make sure to evaluate their time management skills. This is particularly important when the job position being filled will require self-regulation. You want to hire self-starters with good self-discipline. Ask appropriate questions such as "How good are you at setting deadlines and meeting them?" When checking references, as previous employers about time management skills.

All of your employees should be working at their fullest capability. Down-sizing over the previous years has lead to the elimination of many assistant positions and managers and executives are now forced to do their own clerical tasks. If they are performing these tasks on such a regular basis that it would be more cost-effective to hire an *hourly employee*, do so.

When an employee demonstrates above average time management skills, reinforce their actions. In other words, reward them for good behavior. Behavior that is noticed and pleasantly remembered is much more likely to be repeated. In addition, other employees will follow their example.

If you are a good time manager and have good organizational skills, share them with those around you. Teach them how to manage their time. You might begin by asking all employees to bring paper and a pen to meetings in order to take notes. This way they can transfer the items from your assignment list to their to-do list. Arrange meetings in which you refer back to the tasks that were given to them.

Meetings must be conducted in a time-conscious manner. An unorganized meeting can be one of the biggest drains a company has on productivity. If you have trouble believing this, calculate the wages you are paying all the people who are sitting in your next meeting. Meetings should begin on time. Otherwise, people will get into the habit of being late. You should have an agenda. However, be flexible enough so that intellectual breakthroughs can occur. End the meeting after all of your goals have been addressed. Do not let it drag on any further than necessary. Let attendees begin work on the items discussed in the meeting instead of continuing to just talk about them.

Lastly, emphasize how important good time management is to the success of your organization. You could include time management tips in your newsletter. If your company does not have a newsletter, present these tips at staff meetings. Provide time management training opportunities for your employees. Purchase books and CD's on the subject and make them available for use. Conduct on-site organization seminars. Provide employees with personal organizers, whether manual or electronic. Making organization and time management visible at the work place will remind employees of the importance of these skills.

Time is a constant. When poor organizational skills lead to wasted time, this time cannot be retrieved. Each person in an organization needs to evaluate where their time is going on any given day and then implement a few time saving methods to overcome their biggest time wasters. Implementation of too many techniques at one time can result in an employee spending more time organizing than working or becoming overwhelmed and just returning to their old ways out of frustration.

There are numerous time wasters in the work place. Indecision and procrastination are perhaps the two biggest offenders. However, they are closely followed by inefficiency, interruptions, unnecessary errors, crisis management, poor organization, ineffective meetings, micro-managing, failure to delegate, and lack of policies, procedures, or standards to be followed.

Now, let's take a look at some time savers in the workplace. Implementing a few of these techniques can greatly increase productivity and in turn morale. After identifying your time wasters, try to recapture some of that wasted time.
The key to organization and time management is balance.

Life consists of seven areas: health, family, financial, intellectual, social, professional, and spiritual. Although you will not spend equal amounts of time on each of these areas, if you neglect any of them and you will jeopardize your success in all of them.

Next, write things down – whether in a Day Planner or a smartphone. The actual process of writing down a task helps you more easily remember that you need to accomplish it. You are also able to see the big picture and evaluate where the new task fits in with others you already have been assigned.

Plan each day's work and then stick to your plan. If you do not have a plan you will be easily distracted and, therefore, less productive. You will spend your work day responding to others, their requests and crisis situations, rather than completing your own tasks.

When you are planning a day's work, prioritize. Your list of things to be accomplished will include those that are crucial and those that can wait. Make sure you do not spend all your time working on tasks that really aren't as important just because they are smaller and easier to complete. Work your list in order of importance. Do no procrastinate. If you are tempted to put an item off, break down the task into smaller manageable pieces.

According to Dr. Donald E. Wetmore, the average person gets 50 interruptions a day that take about five minutes a piece. This means that we spend over four hours each day dealing with unplanned events. Sorting through the deluge of paper that crosses your desk in a single day can be exhausting. Between e-mail printouts, telephone messages, mail, memos, advertisements, and faxes, your work area can quickly become overwhelming. Try to stick to the rule of handling each item only once. If you don't need it, get rid of it. If you can't handle it in a few minutes, consider delegating it. If it is your responsibility and will take time to address, schedule it on your calendar and put it away.

Get into a routine. Good routines can increase energy and save time, while mindless routines can curb creativity. Make sure any routines you use are serving a purpose other than just to fill up time. Plan times to accomplish certain tasks every day. Repetitive tasks, such as answering email or completing paper work, can be scheduled to be completed during a certain time period each day. This will allow you to devote your full attention to these tasks once a day, instead of partially addressing them several times a day. Set start and stop times for all major tasks during your day.

Make sure you do not take on more than you can handle. You may want to impress your boss, but it can be a mistake to say yes to too many things. You can only accomplish a finite amount of work during the day and taking on more than this will result in the parts of your life becoming imbalanced.

Every time you take something home from work that you said you would do but just didn't quite finish, some area of your personal life is suffering.

Do not put extra effort into tasks that are not worth it. Some tasks will require your full attention and should be completed to the best of your ability. However, there are other tasks that just have to get done. Don't let perfectionism get in the way of completing less important tasks quickly so that you have more time to devote to those projects that really deserve it.

Stephen Covey in <u>First Things First</u> tells the following story:

> One day an expert in time management was speaking to a group of business students. As he stood in front of the group of high-powered overachievers he said, "Okay, time for a quiz." He then pulled out a one-gallon, wide-mouthed Mason jar and set it on the table. He produced about a dozen fist-sized rocks and carefully placed them one at a time into the jar. When the jar was filled to the top and no more rocks would fit inside,

he asked, "Is this jar full?" Everyone in the class said, "Yes." Then he said, "Really?"

He reached under the table and pulled out a bucket of gravel. Then he dumped some gravel in and shook the jar causing it to work down into the space between the big rocks. The he asked the group once more, "Is the jar full?" By this time the class was on to him. "Probably not," one of them answered. "Good!" he replied.

He reached under the table and brought out a bucket of sand and started dumping the sand in the jar until it filled the spaces left between the rocks and the gravel. Once more he asked the question, "Is this jar full?" "No!" the class shouted. Once again he said, "Good."

Then he grabbed a pitcher of water and began to pour it in until the jar was filled to the brim. Then he looked at the class and asked, "What is the point of this illustration?" One eager beaver raised his hand and said, "The point is, no matter how full your schedule is, if you try really hard you can always fit some more things in it!" "No," the speaker replied, "that's not the point."

"The truth this illustration teaches us is that if you don't put the big rocks in first, you'll never get them in at all. What are the 'big rocks' in your life: your children, your loved ones, your education, your dreams, a worthy cause, teaching others, doing things that you love, your health, your mate? Remember to put these BIG ROCKS in first or you'll never get them in at all. If you sweat about the little stuff then you'll never have the real quality time you need to spend on the big, important stuff."

Now that we have looked at the big picture, let's take a look at your own personal work environment and how organizing it can save you time. Look at your desk. Is it cluttered? You should only have eight to nine things on your work surface at any one time. Items used on a daily basis should be kept within reach, but those that are use every other day or less frequently can be relegated to nearby drawers. Items that you may only need weekly or monthly can be stored in a supply closet.

Filing must be done on a regular basis. It is okay to keep a file out that you need to use within the next two days, but anything else should be returned as soon as possible. You are wasting time looking for files when you allow them to stack up in your work area and, in turn, others are unable to access them at all. Set discard dates for all your paper and computer files. These dates may be regulated by law depending what type of industry you are working in so make sure you check if there are any laws governing file retention.

Make a spot on your desk just for incoming items. Label it and make others aware of it. You might even wish to put an inbox on the wall outside your door. This will further reduce interruptions to your busy day.

Keep a master calendar which lists deadlines for all the projects you are currently working on. You don't have to remember everything. Writing down deadlines and appointments not only frees your mind to deal with other problems, it gives you a visual image of what your days and weeks look like. Keeping everything in one place allows you to refer to it easily.

Finally, improving your telephone skills can improve your productivity. When you have to leave a message, make sure to speak slowly and clearly. Give your number at the beginning and the end of the message.   Even when you are leaving a message for a repeat customer, do not assume that they already have your number. If you have an unusual name, spell it.

Following these tips will greatly increase your chances of getting a response to your message. Since you make business phone calls to procure some sort of information that is necessary for the completion of a task, it is vital that your calls be returned.

Your Worth

What is the value of your time? Seems like a simple answer. But if you are using how much money you make as your yardstick and dividing it by a unit measure of time, say an hour, you could be dramatically undervaluing your time.

In order to evaluate how you are using your time, make a list of everything you did today.
Now place a value on each activity. If you answered the telephone, and normally pay someone to do this, use that value. If you made a management decision, place a value on the time it took and multiply that by the worth of a person with such experience and knowledge, you would have to be paying in that position to make that same decision.

Place no value on anything non productive. Try doing the last few days. You may need more rows. Now how much are you presently worth every day?

Activity	Time Spent	Times Value	Total
		Day's Total	

Compare this to how much you are actually making. Are you utilizing your time and skills to their full dollar potential?

Now figure out your optimum hourly value, from the highest hour or most productive position. Multiply this times the total number of hours you evaluated. What is the difference between your optimum value and present worth?

Instead of placing a value on your time, try valuing each task you perform.

Chapter 2 Time Estimation

Engineers and construction estimators spend countless hours using complicated mathematical equations to estimate the time for completion of billion dollar projects. Although missing deadlines can sometimes cost millions of dollars per day, these projects repeatedly run over budget due to miscalculations. If these experts who are paid to estimate project time often fall short, how can a business manager ever hope to estimate project time?

In order to schedule appointments, projects, processes, tasks, and meetings, you need some time estimating skills.

Experience
How long did this same task take the last time? What is the difference between now and the last time this task or project was performed? Have personnel, processes, logistics, or technology change?

Reference
How many references can you collect?

Time estimates from outsourced contractors, product delivery estimates, employee input, etc.

Dependent Factors
What things or people is this task or project dependent on?
Are suppliers manufacturing components that need to be shipped? Are you outsourcing parts of the project?
Components
Break a project into parts and estimate the time each one will take.

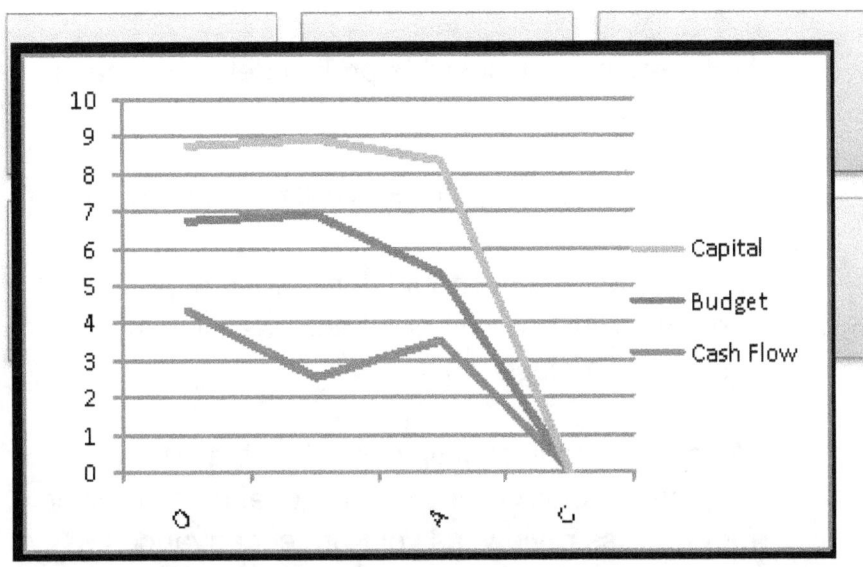

See the Unforeseen
Make a list of unforeseen circumstances that could delay your project. Create a recovery plan for each one. Now estimate the time and cost of these situations.

Project Estimation

Budget
How will money affect the project?

Will there be any possible project delays for cash flow reasons?

If cash flow is reduced when will Capital run out?

Ideally, the budget should deplete the capital required from cash on hand and cash flow by the end of the project.

Also allow additional time for planning. Many projects and tasks require additional planning time for progress review, as your project advances. Include the time you estimate for additional planning.

Include the time for acquiring and additional personnel or outsourcing you will need.

Chapter 3 Plan Your Time

If you haven't got the time to do it right the first time, when will you have the time to do it again?

Schedule Planning Time
Make a weekly planning appointment with yourself. A great time for this appointment in a typical workweek is at the end of the week. This will give you the opportunity to plan the coming week. Fridays are great. You will leave for the weekend with a feeling of confidence and arrive Monday with direction.

For most business owners that are not used to effective time management practices, planning takes intense concentration. That is completely understandable.
Most business owners are flying in combat. They are flying by the seat of their pants throughout most of the day at high speed while being fired at by a barrage of interruptions, while trying to stay in flight and navigating their craft. They have a dozen projects on their minds, fires to extinguish, and new ideas to implement.

Planning boils down an entire week of activity into two hours of concentrated scheduling. Laying out such a strategic blueprint of activity can at first even be painful
and seem non productive. But the rewards of persistent planning with the skills as outlined can be dramatic.

The Three Faces of Time

In order to effectively manage your time, you need to first categorize time. These are not types of activities but rather the types of time available to you.
Prime time is the time you have to be the most productive.

Secondary Time - This is the time you have between prime time and tertiary time.

Secondary time is often
chosen to be spent as prime time or tertiary time.

Tretiary time is the time you spend replenishing.

Prime Time
 This is the time in which you have
to perform whatever it is you do that
produces your livelihood. If you
work from 9 to 5, that is your prime

Secondary Time
 This is the time you have between
prime time and tertiary time.
Secondary time is often
chosen to be spent as prime time or
tertiary time.

Tertiary Time
This is the time you spend in
replenishment. Eating, exercising,
sleeping, relaxing, and bathing, etc.
Tertiary time is often the most
spent time, and is necessary to
support prime and secondary time.

The principle of the Three Faces of Time is based on a productive lifestyle.

While these three faces of time have definite dividing lines, some overlap and occur sporadically. A business lunch could be prime time and tertiary time.

Get OUT!
Optimum Use of Time (OUT) is time spent toward reaching our purpose in the best possible way. This use of time differs for as many purposes and goals people have, so OUT varies for everyone.

So first determine what is your OUT.

For example, an outside sales person's OUT might be spent by being if front of prospects (people.)

Secondly, you must know when your prime time is. When is the best time of the day and the best days to reach your OUT?

A salesperson selling to businesses would probably have a prime time between 9 to 5, Monday through Friday. This person only produces new business when selling face to face. So this salesperson should be in front of business decision makers every minute in prime time. Obviously with travel, planning, scheduling, checking on product deliveries, and following up with customers, spending every second selling to prospects is not feasible. But this salesperson could maximum OUT by:

- Doing as many OUT *Support Activities* as possible outside of prime time hours, such as entering orders, planning, and scheduling after 5PM.

- Scheduling appointments in a desirable geographic sequence.

- Simultaneous Work – (Multitasking) Placing calls while traveling,

As much time as possible should be spent in prime time for your OUT.

In order to define your personal OUT make a list of everything you do that directly helps you reach your goals (productive time).

Then make a second list of OUT support activities. In our example, a salesperson, planning, setting appointments, filling orders, etc. would

Move as many OUT support activities to secondary time slots as possible.

Your Time Budget

Most business owners watch their money closely. They examine profit and loss statements, balance sheets, credit card statements, and their bank balance. They measure cash flow, shop for the best interest rates, bargain for goods, and develop forecasts and budgets. Yet rarely any of these same business owners track and budget their time!

As you go through each day, track your time by making an entry next to each appointment and task scheduled, recording how much time each one actually consumed. Time tracking will give you a record of exactly how you are spending your time.

At the end of the first month, total all the time you schedule for tasks and events. Then total all the time you actually spent accomplishing these tasks. Subtract the actual time spent from the total time allotted. The results will be your time profit or loss.

Make a Time Profit or Loss Statement

This answer will give you some idea how you should be budgeting your time. Eventually, you will have an educated summary of how much time you waste and the amount of time many of your varied tasks actually take.

Tracking Your Time
Enter how much time each scheduled task takes during your day. Be sure to make notes of any interruptions.
Label tasks and appointments as OUT or as OUT support activity. Categorize these tasks and assignments by primary, secondary, or tertiary time.

At the end of each week, use this information to:
- Evaluate what percentage of your time is spent in each area of your time

- See what percentage of your activities is important and what is urgent
- Discover the ratio between planned and unplanned activities
- Spot interrupters and time stealers
- Find out how much time your usual tasks actually take
- Adjust time estimating for future tasks
- Make decisions regarding projects, workflow, and delegation.
- Eliminate unneeded tasks.
- Better organize time and tasks.

Following Your Plan

A plan relieves you of responsibility and energizes you.

Eliminating Procrastination
Most people procrastinate occasionally. Some people procrastinate about almost everything, while some people procrastinate about certain projects or tasks.
Some people believe they work better under pressure. This is almost always a fallacy. People

applying this pressure to their lives most always perform below their potential.

Chronic procrastination can lead to undue stress and even depression, and often requires behavioral changes.

In order to change habits of procrastination, you must determine why you procrastinate.

There are three major reasons for procrastination:

1. PERFECTIONISM

Many procrastinators tend to be perfectionists. When faced with anything too challenging they can become paralyzed and shut down.

2. EMOTIONAL AVOIDANCE

The emotions associated with a particular chore can be overwhelming. Many people avoid the task to avoid the emotion.

3. FEAR

Fear can be paralyzing. Fear of other's reactions, fear of change, fear of risk, and even fear of success can immobilize some people.

If you are procrastinating, indentify the emotions with the task. Is the fear healthy? What is your gut telling you?
Maybe the task is one you should not be doing.

Here are some tips on how to stop dragging your feet:

- Try imagining the task completed. How do you feel?
- Talk to the person or people involved. Ask them how your procrastination is affecting them.
- Try breaking the task down into pieces and doing a part each day.
- Put the task on your schedule.
- Avoid other procrastinators.
- Start a 'no procrastination' program. Set a deadline for every task.

Rather than trying to maintain awareness of, or remember each chore or task you must complete throughout the day –

Trust the clock to be your task manager.

Most business owners that spend the time planning have the best intentions of following their plans. But phone calls, emails, employees, crisis, clients, customers, and vendors all seem to disrupt even the best aspirations.

After a short time of watching their plans disintegrate, they become discouraged and abandon planning time altogether. They are convinced plans simply do not work and conclude time spent planning is a waste of time.

Every plan needs protection.

How To Protect Your Plan

If you spent several hours creating your plan, why would you disrespect yourself and your time by allowing others to destroy it?

Protecting your plan is about learning how to respect your own time. Your time is your life. Your prime time is your money.

Avoid Interruptions – Do not answer your phone during certain time blocks in your plan. If you must heed these calls, at least limit them by screening with either your employees or caller ID. Do not allow email pop-ups while working at your computer. (More on interruptions in the next Chapter.)

Schedule Reactive Activity – Set appointments during the day when you will read and respond to email, when you will answer telephones, when you will take interruptions!

Have A Plan B – This might be one the greatest time savers you will ever use. No matter how well you plan, things happen that you will have no control over, events or occurrences that suddenly give you unplanned time. Your appointment might not show, you could be kept waiting for an appointment, or an employee could be late. Keep productive activities available as a plan B to substitute at any given time.

Keep Meeting Times – Start meetings promptly and always give the ending time the same precise attention. Follow meeting plans.

Be Prepared – Schedule time between activities to prepare for the next activity.

Be Realistic – Be as accurate as possible about the amount of time you allot for activities.

Break Yourself In – While most business owners are optimistic with great expectations, if you are not used to following a schedule, start slow. Leave yourself those times during the day when you need to think or get away.

Make it a Team Effort and Inform Others – Make sure employees, clients, vendors, co-workers, and other associates know you are going to be following a new schedule. You might be surprised how many people will help you protect your plan.

Create Expectations – Train others about what they should expect from you. Let them know a sense of urgency exists in business. Show up early, start meetings and appointments on time, get to the point, and conclude and leave on time.

Respect Others – Showing up late or keeping people waiting is disrespectful. Disrespecting other's time is impudent. Time is the very substance of life. Keeping people waiting for appointments and meetings, does not show you are important. It shows you are impolite. If you want people to respect your time, start by respecting theirs.

Be Generous - Give Others Specific Time – Give people regular and specific times when you are available for impromptu meetings or conversations. Those people who might be used to 'popping in' throughout your day who might sometimes have important information will continue to communicate with you especially if they know they will have their own time slot. Be strict but give them time to adjust to your schedule.   (This does not mean you should surrender to any negative time wasters.)

Blame it on the Clock! – When people have reached the end of their appointment or time slot, simply state, "The clock says I have to go now," or "According to the clock, I have to get to my next meeting." This gets you off the hook, and you'll find most people will not object – it's hard to argue with the clock!

After you have determined where your time is going, you can then create goals to rid yourself of your own person time wasters. Set goals and keep track of whether or not you are accomplishing them. Use organizational tools to help you complete your goals. You may prefer a Day Planner, a software program such as Microsoft Outlook, or a smartphone app. Whatever tool you choose to use, prioritize each day's tasks. Determine what tasks must be done today, what your long-term deadlines are, and what things need to be accomplished in the future.

Reevaluate this list as necessary. Always leave time in your schedule for the unexpected. Twenty to thirty hours of your week should be devoted to specific tasks. However, attempt to leave around ten hours free for the unexpected. You never know when you will need more time on a project than you expect or when a personal issue may arise that must be addressed.

Chapter 4 Take Control of Your Time

Prioritizing Tasks
The ability to choose and complete tasks in the order of importance highly desirable and more challenging for some business types than others.

In order to choose tasks you must be aware of as many chores and projects as possible. In order to do this, every planning session must have a list.

You Must Have a List!

List all your tasks, then rate them, and list them again in order. Then you can schedule them. When all tasks and projects are rated, use these additional filters to prioritize:

- Imagine the consequences of eliminating the task. – This exercise will often remove some unneeded tasks altogether.
- Decide if each task should be performed in prime time or secondary time.
- Determine who will be affected by the task.

Now Reduce Your List
Until we can effectively clone ourselves to be in more than one place at a time, most of us need to reduce our workload.
Before you start prioritizing, consider these task elimination criteria:

Does This Task or Project Make Sense?
Every task you do should first have to pass this benchmark.
You have goals, priorities, and objectives. Does every task contribute to your big picture? Estimate how much time each task will take, then imagine what you would do with the time if the task were cancelled. While not always possible, everything you do should contribute to your objectives.

Why is the Task Urgent?
While urgency should be a mindset of business, urgency should also be questioned – *ruthlessly*.
Is the urgency only appeasing someone else?
What has caused the urgency? Many urgent situations have been caused by mistakes.
Determining the cause of urgency can eliminate or postpone a task and lead to prevention measures of interruptions and mistakes.

Some seemingly imperative tasks are not urgent at all. Customers might be making demands that are unnecessary.
Check with all parties involved.

The Delegation Qualifier
Are you the only person that can handle the task? Sometimes you might be, but many times someone else can perform for you. Delegate everything possible to free up your schedule.

How Else Could the Task Be Done?
  Are You Utilizing Technology
Could an in person appointment be a phone call? Conference calling can rule out travel and save an enormous amount of time.
Could you email instead of calling?
Email can be done on your terms when you want. You will have time to articulate better compared to the live telephone conversation. Time can be wasted and sales lost by leaving phone messages for people. Email eliminates phone tag.
  Can the Task Be Dissected?
Are there portions of the work that can be delegated, eliminated, or postponed?

What is the Cost of Excluding a Task?
There are many jobs throughout the day that are actually not worth the time to do. Applying the dollar figure when considering cancelling a task is another measure of the task value.

The Measures of Task Value

Money – How much is the task worth?
Time – How much time will it take?
Effect – Completed versus Cancelled
Effectiveness – What is the most effective way to perform the task?
Contribution to Your Objectives
Replacement – (What could be done with the time instead?)
Division- Dividing the Task Into Parts
When – Can the task be performed just as well in secondary time?

One great trick for prioritizing is to give *every* task a deadline.

Give tasks a deadline.

While many business owners define a start time for projects and tasks when planning, they do not establish a deadline. Having a clear deadline makes tasks easier to prioritize.

Prioritizing while planning is easy. You have time to think. Prioritizing while working is a bit more challenging.

Prioritizing Interruptions
While most people are familiar with prioritizing tasks, few people prioritize their interruptions. Hence, few people have defined the types of events that interrupt them.

Define Interruption Types

In order to take control of your time, you must minimize interruptions. Many people describe their positions as managers, and define management as 'putting out fires,' or solving problems. While having a job definition for yourself is a great start, most owners have not defined or classified these problems. They just catch every ball tossed at them. The tail is often wagging the dog.

49

Think about how you are interrupted from your OUT
or productive work. Make a list of every kind of
interruption you have experienced in the last three
months.

People
Employees
Clients
Customers
Vendors
Prospects

Devices
Email
Telephone
Blackberry

Processes
Electrical Outage
Cash Flow Short
Supplies

Minimizing Interruptions

People Interruptions

Employee Interruptions

Tell managers and key personnel you cannot be disturbed unless it is an emergency. Define to them what an emergency is by making a list of specific examples. Be very clear as the word emergency is open to broad definition. Some people classify an emergency only as fire or pending death. Others consider a paper jam in the copier a crisis.

Then schedule appointments daily or weekly with each person, based on how often they presently communicate with you. If your manager is accustom to talking with you throughout the day, dedicate a time just for talking. If each person knows they have this appointed time, and a precise understanding of an emergency, they will be less likely to interrupt you.

Customers and Clients

Business owners have often unknowingly trained customers and clients to interrupt them. While service to customers is an utmost concern, customers come to expect the type of service you provide. Their expectations have often been set by your business. They might be used to having free access to you by phone at any time, or having you respond instantly or within a certain amount of time.

When planning your week, if you set aside a time each day or as needed, to respond to telephone calls and emails, let your clients or customers know.

> Set standards to aid in the control
> of other's behavior.

Define for yourself what client emergencies are and which ones you will respond to.

Family
You can do the same thing with family members. If your spouse has a habit of communicating during your OUT, discuss emergency situations and set appointments at usual intervals to talk.

Many times this will make a spouse feel an additional sense of importance, knowing you are dedicating specific time to them.

Devices
Most devices that interrupt us are actually human interruptions. The good news here is we are in control of these devices. They can all be temporarily shut off.

Processes
Select the interruptions from your list that are process oriented. Now divide then into preventable and unpreventable.

Many process interruptions can be prevented. Running short on inventory, running out of supplies, computer viruses, etc. With a bit of planning and implementing new measures, you should be able to eliminate most of these interruptions types.

Some process interruptions are not preventable. Electrical outages, equipment breakdowns, cash flow shortages, etc.

Many unpreventable business interruptions can be 'cured.'

- Electrical outages can be cured by backup generators.

- Equipment breakdowns can be cured by backing up computers, having backup equipment or keeping a cash fund for replacing equipment, or having dependable technical help contacts, on staff, or on retainer.

- Cash flow shortages can be cured by having credit cards, cash reserves, or a line of credit established.

Tracking Interruptions

Interruption	People	Process	Device	Time Lost
Totals				

Total your times and chart your interruptions.

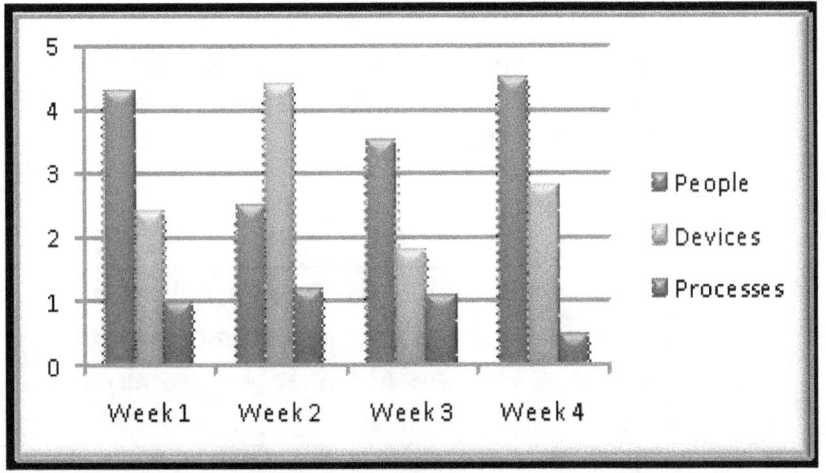

After you have carted your interruptions for a four week period, you'll have a pretty good idea, where they are coming from.

Remember you cannot stop all interruptions or always control people's behavior, but as in the title of this chapter, you can 'Minimize' interruptions to take more control of your time.

Identifying Time Stealers and Arresting Them

How much of your work day is actually productive?
Most of us spend countless number of hours on
repeating tasks we have already done, reacting to
situations that should never have arisen, and
ranting about how much we have to do and what
little time we have to do them in. In order to figure
out where all our time is going we have to become
aware of our actions.

Keep a journal of what you do with the time you
spend at work for at least one week. This can be
extremely tedious and seem to take up even more
of your precious time, but in order to improve time
management we have to become aware of where
our time goes. As the Roman philosopher Seneca
said, you tend to use "time as if you had more and
more forever."

After you have completed your log, analyze it. Look
for time stealers. Time stealers are anything that
reduces your effectiveness in the workplace.
Examples include: doing work that you should
have delegated, spending too much time answering
or sending email, unnecessary telephone

conversations, interruptions by other employees, long-winded meetings, rushing through projects that should have been completed at an earlier date, trying to accomplish too many things at once, redoing other people's work because it is not up to par, doing tasks more than once, lack of skills or knowledge, poor planning, lack of sleep, inability to say "no", and lack of a plan for your day.
Where does your time go?

Many business owners get so caught up in the day-to-day running of their businesses that they just don't realize where their time goes. Before they know it, it's 6:00pm and if you ask them what they have achieved they probably couldn't tell you.

The first step in sorting out your time management problems is to identify where your time goes – keep a log of what you do and when you do it.

Complete that for a week or two.

After you have compiled your log, take a look at it and identify the most frequent time stealers that reduce your effectiveness in the workplace.

These could include:

- Doing work that others should be completing
- Answering emails/too many emails coming in
- Telephone interruptions that should not have got through
- Interruptions from staff that could have gone elsewhere
- Unnecessary meetings
- Tasks that you should have delegated
- Tasks and decisions that you have been putting off
- Getting involved in the "doing" too much
- Putting out fires
- Poor communication
- Duplication of work
- Lack of skills or knowledge
- Lack of planning
- Tiredness
- Can't say NO
- No system to organize your day

All is not lost, however. You can reclaim your time!

Here are 10 techniques and strategies that you can use to manage your time more effectively.

Top 10 Time Management Tips

1. COMPLETE A BUSINESS AUDIT EACH MONTH

Take a look at your business and make a note of your top priorities for each day/week/month. Make a decision on where you want to focus your energy and then look at everything else you have been doing and decide what to do with it.

2. DON'T SWEAT THE SMALL STUFF

Work out what areas you add the most value to the business and make a decision that at least 80 per cent of your time will be spent on these activities.

3. DELEGATE

Let go of the reins and delegate your work more often. Whatever task you do from now on ask yourself "Should I really be doing this?" and "Can someone else do this instead?"

4. OUTSOURCE

You and your staff do not need to do everything you know! Nike doesn't actually make shoes! Could you outsource some of your tasks and operation to a third party outsider?

5. PERSONAL ORGANIZATION

Make proper use of TO DO lists and your diary – make using them a habit. Can you automate any tasks like getting email on your mobile phone?

6. PROCESS IMPROVEMENT

By simplifying your business and your processes you can make it a lot easier to run and this in turn will lead to saving you a lot of time.

7. IMPROVE YOUR COMMUNICATION SKILLS

You will get the most out of your staff and save yourself a lot of time in the process if you can communicate what you want in a clear, concise manner. Assertiveness skills will also allow you to say "NO" in the right way to requests and will allow you to manage the frequent interruptions that you get on a daily basis.

8. FOCUS ON STRATEGY

Know where you are heading and why you want to get there. This will keep you focused on what is important. Continually revisit your strategy to make sure you keep on track and away from all of the distractions.

9. IMPORTANT AND URGENT TASKS ARE NOT THE SAME

As soon as you can make this distinction you will be able to categorize your tasks accordingly and know what to do with each one.

Source: Covey's Time-Management Matrix - Stephen Covey's
The 7 Habits of Highly Effective People.

	Urgent	Not Urgent
Important	I ➤ Crises ➤ Pressing problems ➤ Firefighting ➤ Major scrap and rework ➤ Deadline-driven projects	II ➤ Prevention ➤ *Production capability* activities ➤ Relationship building ➤ Recognizing new opportunities ➤ Planning ➤ *Re*-creation
Not Important	III ➤ Interruptions ➤ Some calls ➤ Some mail ➤ Some reports ➤ Some meetings ➤ Proximate pressing matters ➤ Popular activities ➤ Some scrap & rework	IV ➤ Trivia ➤ Busywork ➤ Some mail ➤ Some phone calls ➤ Time-wasters ➤ Pleasant activities

10. KEEP ON IT!

Keep analyzing where you are spending your
time on a monthly basis and make adjustments to
what you should be doing and how you are doing it.
We all stray off track from time to time so don't beat

yourself up about it, just take stock and move forward.

Now that you know what your particular time stealers are, how do you arrest them? In most cases, people have to come to terms with the fact that they cannot do everything but that they can do what is most important. Planning and goal setting is of the utmost importance.

The Breakup

Projects often can be overwhelming. Most small businesses overbook projects to keep the income hopper full.

Break your projects into parts and at times delegate these parts to colleagues. When you delegate a task, however, make sure you communicate clearly what results you desire, *what the deadline is*, and all the necessary instructions that the person will need to complete the project. Make sure that you verify that the person understands of what is expected of them. As each part of the project is accomplished, recognize your successes and build on them.

Behavioral Changes For Effective Time Management

- Clarify your goals. Revise them monthly. Stay aware of them daily. Keep a list where you will see them daily.

- Don't rely on your memory only. Keep information in trusted system where you can organize and classify it.
- Plan your day each week the week before and each morning the night before. You should have clear to do list for every workday.
- Set exact deadlines – date and even time, if necessary.
- Create a system to notify yourself of scheduled tasks.
- Prioritize and focus.
- Continually evaluate your progress at the end of the day.
- Look ahead for a week, a month, and a year at a time.
- Examine your habits. If they are harmful or useless, get rid of them.
- Avoid procrastination by scheduling every task. If anything must be postponed – reschedule immediately.
- Eliminate mediocre projects.
- Reward yourself when you get things done as you have planned, especially, if these things are important to you.

- Always have a Plan B - If you are delayed or waiting for something or somebody, make use of this time.
- Ruthlessly analyze your time and search for new time management opportunities.
- Delegate responsibilities and tasks whenever possible.
- Ask for advice when you need it.
- Keep negative people out of your environment.
- Enjoy yourself. Be optimistic and positive about your life.

Meetings

In a recent survey, sixty two per cent of business owners and personnel listed meetings as the number one source of wasted time.

- Create an agenda and rules for your meetings. Send everyone a copy before they attend.

- Have a start time and ending time for meetings. Set a lock out time within two minutes of start time and exclude the late arrivals. You might need to hold a few dry run meetings to get employees accustom to this new rule. Do not tell anyone these are practice meetings.

- In company group meetings, set time limit on speaking. Give one a timer and instruct them to hold up a 'Time's Up' sign when the limit has been reached.

- Make sure attendees are really necessary to the meeting.

- Avoid meetings when other forms of communication will suffice.

- Use technology for teleconferencing, etc. when possible instead of traveling.

- Have an out – or exit strategy. Have an appointment or other use for the room that must start promptly at your meetings scheduled ending time.

Multitasking

In our new world of overburdened workloads, multitasking has become a coined word representing more achievement by performing multiple tasks.

But multitasking requires multi- ASKING.
When is multitasking really effective?

With more techno-gadgets available than ever before, multitasking has become the norm. A common form of mutli-tasking, a business meeting over lunch, accomplishes productive time during a secondary time activity and can be greatly beneficial.

Talking on the phone with a supplier while simultaneously emailing a customer can be tricky and detrimental. Talking on the phone, while driving, can perilous.

Is your multitasking effective?
Most people do not perform either task as well when multitasking. Ask yourself before trying to perform two or more tasks at the same time.

Make a list of all your multi-tasking activities. Look at each one individually and compare your effectiveness to performing each one solo.

Limit Incoming Attacks
Shut off your email notification and let your phone go to voice mail. Take a fifteen minute break during the day away from everything. Go for a walk around the block without your cell phone. Sit outside on a park bench. Some place where you can be completely uninterrupted for fifteen minutes. Let your mind come to a halt. The renewed energy from such a break can make you more effective and less stressed.

Establish Rules for Your Time
When creating your schedule establish a set of rules for your time. Turn off your cell phone during secondary time, for example during dinner. Decide when what and when you will not multitask. Set blocks of time aside when you are unavailable to people and devices.

Review

Top Ten Ways to Stick to Your Plan

1. Avoid interruptions
2. Schedule reactive activity
3. Have a Plan B
4. Keep Meeting Times
5. Be Prepared
6. Be Realistic
7. Break Yourself In
8. Make it a Team Effort
9. Be Generous
10. Blame it on the clock

Chapter 5 The Cleanest Dirty Word - *Organization*

Organizational Skills for Business Owner's

Are you working too hard because you just can't seem to get organized? Organizational skills are perhaps the most undervalued trait of successful business men and women. Today's business environment requires its leaders to manage the incredible amount of information from different sources they are inundated with each day and to be able to process it effectively.

Organization must be addressed at both a corporate and a personal level. The members of a corporate team must be able to work well together, plan ahead, and concentrate on one or two major goals. They must communicate well by sharing their schedules and updating both personal and client contact information on a regular basis.

Workspace
Workspaces must be organized in order for all employees to have easy access to resources on an as needed basis. If just one person does not re-file

important documents or place them where they can be re-filed, the entire office's productivity will suffer. When was the last time you cleaned your virtual desktop? Most computer desktops are cluttered with icons and folders within folders and file names with variations.

When an employee is absent, production can come to a halt for the lack of a password. Keep an updated master list of passwords in a safe but accessible location.

Process Organization
Another area in which an organization can save time is processing mail. Mail should be opened as soon as it arrives and sorted into piles: Accounts Payable, Checks to be Deposited, and Advertising. Deal with one pile at a time and only deal with each piece of mail once. If you allow these piles to pile up, you can easily miss something important while you're rushing through attempting to get caught up. Remember that you do not need to keep every piece of paper that crosses your desk. The same information is often available elsewhere. For example, bank records are now available online as are magazine articles.

On a more personal level, you can organize your
workspace to allow you to complete tasks more
efficiently. Put yourself in the center of your work
area. Keep a small amount of supplies at hand, but
store large quantities so that they are not in your
way. Clean up as you complete a task. Do not
allow supplies to pile up. Use the tops of filing
cabinets and bookcases to store hardware, such as
printers and scanners. This will free up useable
workspace. Finally, scan and file documents on the
computer, always make a back-up copy and get rid
of the paper version.

This filing method will only be helpful to you if your
organization's computers are utilizing an effective
file management system.

Chapter 6 To Be Or Not To Be – Making Decisions

Business owners waste an enormous amount of time thinking about and making decisions.
Agonizing over decisions can interrupt all Three Faces of Time.
Sleepless nights can violate tertiary time, which can leave you depleted and less productive.

Few business owners have analyzed their own decision making process. What is your decision making process?

- Gather all information about your subject.
- Make sure you have identified the issue or challenge of your decision correctly. look for the cause of issues, not the symptoms.
- Consider the timeliness of your decision.
- Consider the consequences of making no decision.
- Consult others about your decision.
- Make a plan and execute your decision

Decision Making Techniques

Consequence Technique
Imagine the consequences to your decisions, good and bad.

Fantasizing Technique
Many times we limit ourselves to our present position when making decisions. While this is practical, a simple fantasizing technique can open your mind to new ideas.
In order to open your mind to possibilities, try fantasizing about your position. For example, how would you do things differently with an unlimited budget?
What is the optimum or perfect outcome for your decision?

Mentor Technique
When you are up against the wall on a decision, having mentors that you can run things by can make all the difference. Find people that are not involved in the day to day operations of your business, that you trust. These people need not be in your industry, but good decision makers. Make connections and keep in contact, having a list of

such people around saves the time of looking for them in a time of need.

In Their Shoes Technique
Try to imagine the perspective of everyone else involved in the decision and/or affected by the decision. If needed, ask people involved how they believe different decisions will affect them.

Inductive Reasoning
See the big picture and imagine the different outcomes of your decisions. Draw conclusions based on your past experience in similar situations and the experiences of others. Base your hypothesis on as many facts as possible.

Cost Benefit Analysis
Weigh the costs of alternative decisions and estimate the benefits. While all other applicable techniques should be exhausted, this one should be one of the first used.

Benefits and Risks
One systematic decision making approach was developed by Charles Kepner and Bejamin Tregoe. This approach uses a matrix process to force users

to weigh all benefits and risks. Benefits and risks include much more than profit and loss. customer satisfaction, client retention, employee moral, ability to attract skilled employees, loss of employees, cost consequences, and litigation prevention, just to name a few.

The Art of Stopping
In order to avoid jumping to the wrong conclusions, or in order to gather facts, stop and ask, when does this decision need to be made. Consider the consequences of holding off on making a decision. This will give you the time to collect more data and verify information.

Decision Value
Estimate the cost to make a decision. Often, the costs of studies made to reach decisions have been more costly than the outcome of the any choice made. Weigh the time and manpower that will be needed to make the decision. Know the value of making a decision.

Group Consensus

Bring everyone involved together and have a discussion. You could even get a democratic vote from the group to consider the majority opinion.

Pros and Cons
One of the oldest but still reliable decision making strategies. Draw two columns and list the benefits of a decision on one side and the disadvantages on the other. Weigh the results.

Chapter 7 Talk... Talk... Talk

A recent study suggests that the number one time waster in business today is from communication confusion.

<u>Communication Blunders</u>

- Giving Poor Instructions
- Inability to Listen to Instructions
- Causing Personal/Emotional Discord
- Inciting Anger
- Miscommunication of Ideas
- Revealing Proprietary Information
- Irrelevant Communication
- Counter Productive Communication
- Confusing Communication – Mixed Messages
- Lack of Communication
- Inappropriate Communication
- Dishonesty

Time spent expressing ideas, correcting statements, dealing with employee and personal repercussions of miscommunication, time wasted due to poor instructions or inability to listen to instructions,

Communicating More Effectively

Consider the Person

First consider who you are communicating to. Are you putting your message in their terms. Consider their vocabulary, listening ability, and pattern of thinking.

Some people cannot handle more than a few simple instructions at once.

Now consider your method of communication. Some people respond better to verbal instructions, others a written message, while still other people need both.

Ask people to repeat your instructions or communication back to you. You can do this without sounding condescending by saying something like this, "I'm not sure if I really communicated that well, could you tell me what I just said?"

You might get some surprising responses, but this exercise gives you the opportunity to head off misunderstandings before they become counterproductive.

Everyone has filters through which they hear and interpret information. These filters include their level of vocabulary and language, their personal self image, past experiences, their perception of you, and expectations.

Don't assume anything when communicating with others.

Remember to listen well. Most miscommunication can be contributed to poor listening.

Battling Opposition
When met with opposition to your ideas try using creative vocabulary.

Disarm People
How can you make people more receptive to you message?

Whenever possible, set the mood, or control the environment where you communicate. People in a relaxed state of mind are more receptive to listening.

Start conversations in a disarming or neutralizing manner. While many managers and business owners feel chit chat is a waste of time, this can disarm people and put them in a receptive state. In addition, you will often get more and useful information from people when chatting.
 A defensive person usually has reduced listening ability.
They will not hear most of what you say. A person on the defensive will be stopped by the words they find offensive.
You will waste an incredible amount of time breaking down someone in a defensive state.

Allow Time for Questions
In addition to having people repeat your instructions or statements, ask them if they have questions.
In a group setting, allow private time for one on one questions from individuals involved in the group.
This could also be by email. People will often ask questions privately that they would not ask in a

group setting. This could be because they do not want to appear less intelligent in front of their peers. Follow up with people and ask if they need assistance or have questions about a project or task.

Project Communication
The major shortcoming in project management is the difference between expectations and results. This is often due to lack of, misunderstood, or poor communication.

Many people require visual communication to understand concepts.

Chapter 8 Delegation and Outsourcing

Delegating

Know what you are worth…

An old mentor of mine once said:

"If you could take the tasks that you are currently doing that have the biggest impact upon your business in terms of profit and turnover and just do them all day, every day, what would they be and what would the impact be?"

These were wise words!

As soon as I started to only do the tasks that were on a par with or above my hourly rate and gave the rest out to others, my business soared.

The same can be said with business owners.

Many business owners think that by "letting go" of certain tasks or hiring others to do them, it adds to their cost base. Yes, it does add to the cost base but what does an additional 80 per cent of you doing what you are best at generate for your business in terms of turnover and profits?

The effective delegating of tasks is an indispensable skill for owners, and a direct contributor to good time management. Some owners delegate most every task before them, and are still drastically short of time.

Business owners are usually 'take charge' people. They know their businesses better than anyone and can perform most every job. These owners often refuse to let go of tasks below their capabilities, which is not always in the best interest of the business. As if the Captain of the ship refused to give up swabbing the deck, because he felt no one could swab a deck like him, these owners hold on to tasks. Many a business vessel has run aground with clean decks.

As a small business owner, you must decide which jobs would be better off delegated or outsourced. Let go of any duty, which would be better delegated.

Some people might do the job differently than you, but effectively reach the same results.

Question every task in front of you.
Decide who, beside yourself, could perform each one.
If this is difficult, imagine you if you were somehow restricted to only delegating. Who would do your job?

When possible, give employees choices. Ask them to decide what tasks they would like to assume.

If some employees might be more capable in specific areas, consider having employees exchange tasks.

Remember delegating should free you of time. There is a fine line between successful delegating and failure from other's incompetence. Be sure to give eager employees the opportunity to try new responsibilities, but do not delegate tasks that are beyond people's abilities. Consider starting or paying for educational or training programs for ambitious employees.

Be careful about dividing a task among people. Grouping people could create new human management challenges that eradicate any time savings.

Effectively communicate expectations and deadlines for delegated tasks.

Delegated Tasks Checklist

- Put Your Task Plan In Writing and Document Progress
- Clarify your goal. Make sure the person or people understand the desired results.
- Create a visual picture of the expected outcome.
- Determine criteria to analyze results.
- Make results measurable.
- Determine what obstacles delegates might encounter, such as budget restraints, time conflicts, etc.
- Compose a list of actions you have to take in order to achieve your goal. Write down as many ideas as possible.
- Set task milestones and have Mark the most necessary and effective steps by setting them high priority status.
- Keep directions as simple as possible.

- Review the action plan regularly. If you have any new information, make changes in your plan taking it into account.
- Monitor delegated activity. Set task milestones and have people report results to you at critical intervals.

Whenever possible have a Plan B for delegated tasks that fall short of completion or produce undesirable results.

Outsourcing

Many owners have discovered the benefits of outsourcing, from projects to accounting services. The time to locate vendors, check references, evaluate services, collect bids and make payment plans, must be weighed for each service or project.

To get your feet wet try posting a simple job on an online outsourcing service.

Outsourcing Tips

- Don't commit to long-term contracts.
- Make sure you have a clear contract.
- Communicate effectively.
- Define your project clearly.
- Be firm about deadlines
- Be flexible about ideas from vendors.
- Be sure you understand the terms and charges.
- Pay all vendors as promised.

Chapter 9 Time Saving Tools

There are now many aids and types of tools that will save time and increase availability to the business owner.

In this age of techno business and virtual worlds, seems sophisticated electronic devices are procreating morphed generations of themselves incessantly.

Business has been invaded by smartphones, I-pads, bluetooth technology, backup drives, call forwarding, email notification, wireless technology, blogging, and so on.

A quick tutorial in business electronics is needed just to make an educated decision.

Smartphones
Many business owners are already familiar with the advantages of smartphones.
They are small and smart telephones with multiple features that enable you to export and import data, store information, such as address books and

calendars, and make lists. They are great easy-to-use time management tools.

Online Project Boards
Online project boards are great for any task or project involving multiple people or people in multiple locations. It gives you the tools to collaborate and share documents with employees, customers, clients and partners.

What have not changed are the principles of effective time management and skills needed. The basic skills outlined in this book will help you become far more productive. The electronic devices available help measure time, control activity, record, schedule, estimate, and communicate more effectively.

There are several positive byproducts of managing time effectively including: increased confidence, stress relief, improved productivity, and a higher energy level.

RSS Feeds
Business owners like most people are inundated with information and news.

How are you getting your news?
For many years news was either read from a newspaper or seen on a television broadcast. There was little choice as to what news or when. Now with the advent of the Internet, there is much more news, and this news is really current – up to the minute.
But what news really benefits you?

Choose Your News
News can be a major distraction. The majority of news is negative- because that's what sells. What news do you really need to be productive in your business? Choose that news by RSS feed. Filter out everything else. If you feel you really need the latest chit chat and violence, set aside some secondary time to watch the news.

Scanning and Shredding

With all the time lost looking for paperwork, replacing lost paperwork, and the space required, every business should invest the time in scanning documents and records to their computers and shredding all paper that is not absolutely necessary.

While this seems like an elementary concept, few businesses fully utilize digital storage. This is one time saver that does require an initial investment of time, scanning paperwork and destroying. But studies have shown that the time required to file, protect, and retrieve documents is a major cost to Businesses.

Backup Systems

Keep disaster plans in place and practice prevention. With the scheduling software and now available and the low cost of additional hard drives, there is no excuse for not having daily backups of computers.

One computer crash without a back up can cost you more than just the time to recover; it can ruin your business.

Conclusion

The information and strategies in this book can change your bottom line and life!
Start everyday with an accomplishment that energizes you. For some this is a physical workout, others a project. When you start living effective time management you'll feel in control, and have more time for yourself.

Use the tactics in this book to avoid procrastinating.

Don't over schedule yourself. Many business owners attack time management like any other program, with full steam. Scheduling too much in a day will lead to constant changes, delayed projects, and a feeling of overall failure. Start slow and build. Be flexible.

Measure your success with your time logs. Use the time profit or loss statements to make adjustments. Keep lists of the interrupters.

While any change can sometimes feel uncomfortable at first, the rewards of managing yourself effectively are dimensional. You will become more energetic, more profitable, more relaxed, and experience greater confidence.

Make it a point to set an example of your new self management strategy. Tell others about your plans. If everyone throughout your company and customers and clients jump on the band wagon to manage themselves, everyone will benefit.

After you have become accustom to your weekly panning, start making an annual plan.
At the end of every year, take a weekend away to reflect on the past year and make plans for the new one. Make a list of items you wish to accomplish in the upcoming year. Schedule the projects, vacations, and events that you can.

In a world where uncertainty reigns, contemplating the future with an activity plan has a calming effect.

Taking control of your time will give you an 'in charge' feeling and confidence that other's will notice.

Remember that saving time requires an investment of time, the time to plan, make changes, and better manage you.

Are You Ready To Take Your Business To The Next Level?

One-on-One Small Business Coaching and Personal Coaching with Wayne Sutton.

Get your FREE newsletter and marketing tips at www.CoachingWithWayne.com

www.ingramcontent.com/pod-product-compliance
Lightning Source LLC
Chambersburg PA
CBHW051732170526
45167CB00002B/897